COMMUNITY HELPERS SERIES
JENE BARR, Educational Consultant

Wings and Wheels

CYNTHIA CHAPIN
Pictures: Kevin Royt

ALBERT WHITMAN & COMPANY Chicago

PICTURE DICTIONARY

boxcar

bus

caboose

delivery truck

flatcar

freight car

garbage truck

gas pump

© 1967 by Albert Whitman & Company. L.C. Catalog Card 67-17415
Published simultaneously in Canada by George J. McLeod, Ltd., Toronto
Printed in U.S.A.

helicopter

locomotive

passenger

piggyback car

plane

tank car

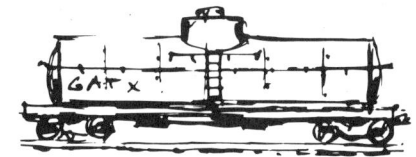

tank truck

taxicab

wheels

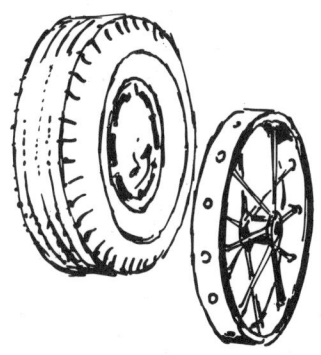

Planes and trains, cars and trucks,
and buses come and go.
They carry books and beds,
and dishes and food,
and all the things we need.
They help us travel far and near.
Such busy wings and wheels!

It's early in the morning.
Sam's Service Station is open.
Here comes a bakery truck
filled with bread and pies and cakes
which must go to many stores.
But first, the driver stops for gas.

Mike and Mary come into the gas station.
They have some coffee for their father.
"How about some rolls with your coffee?"
asks the bakery man.
"With my new truck I can deliver things
hot from the oven."

Mr. Green drives up to the gas pumps.
Four people ride to work with Mr. Green
and home again.
These people have a car pool.
"Fill it up," says Mr. Green.
"We have to get to work on time."

A big trailer truck roars
down the highway.
Its lights are still on.
The truck is filled with watermelons.
"That truck must have been traveling
all night," says Mike.
The truck rushes on to the city.

A garbage truck pulls in at the gas station.
The back of the truck has a lift.
This lift is like an elevator.
It raises the garbage cans
to a helper at the top and then
brings the empty cans down again.

A fire truck races past.
Listen to the siren!
Out of the way—everybody!

Now a big gasoline truck drives in.
The driver fills the tanks in the station with gas.
No one can see the tanks because they are under the ground.

The soft-drink driver comes.
"Did you drink up all the pop?"
he asks Mike and Mary.
The driver fills up the pop machine.

A cab stops for gas.
"Fill it up," says the cab driver.
"I have to drive all the way
to the airport."
Here comes the school bus.
Quick! Mike and Mary get their books
and climb in the bus.

Many buses come and go.
Some buses take people to stores,
then home with their bundles.
They take people to work
or to visit friends.
Some buses carry passengers
to cities far away.

After school, Mike and Mary
ride their bicycles.
Mary rides her bicycle to the store
to get bread for Mother.
Mike is a newsboy.
He rides his bike to deliver papers.

Mike and Mary stop at the gas station.
They watch Father check the tires
on a red car.
Mike and Mary need air for their
bicycle tires, too.
Father says, "That's right!
All drivers should check the air
in their tires. Keep safe!"

Mike and Mary ride past the railroad station.
They see a train stop.
They watch people get off the train.
They see people get on.

A trainman opens the baggage car.
He takes out sacks of mail.
He takes out packages.
Look! He takes out a little dog.
It's a poodle!

A long freight train slows down.
Mike counts 37 cars!
There are refrigerator cars
for meat and fruit and frozen food.
There are tank cars that carry oil,
and there are coal cars.
There are flatcars that carry
farm machines.
And there are piggyback cars
with trailer trucks on them.
Inside the trucks are radios
and toys and TV sets.

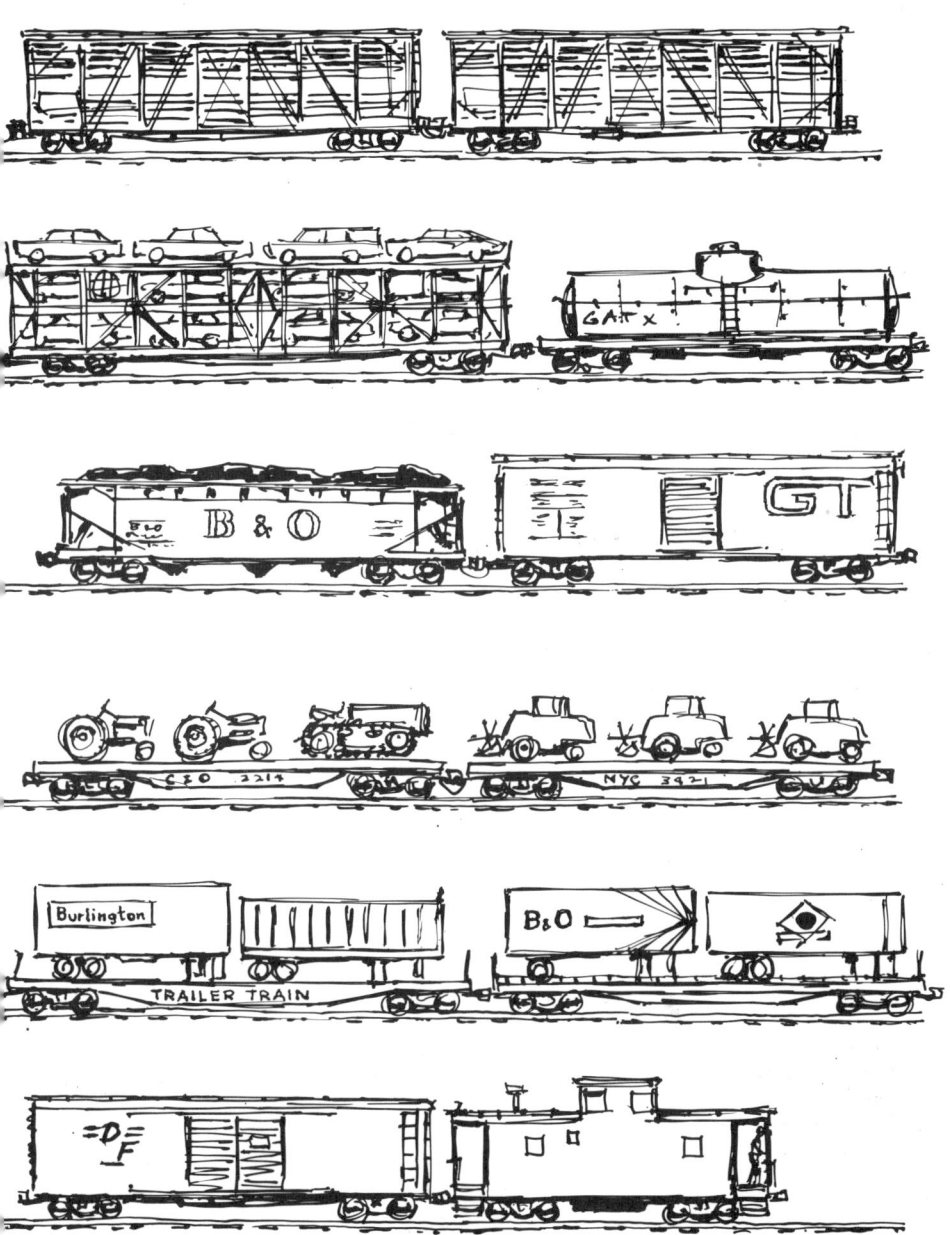

The freight train pulls into
the freight yard.
Trucks stand ready to pull the trailers
down the ramp and off the piggyback cars.
Men hurry to unload the boxcars.
What a busy place!

A big locomotive on another track
pulls away a loaded freight train.
Some cars are filled with wheat
to go to the flour mills.
Some carry lumber to build houses
and make furniture.
And some carry new cars and
station wagons.
The last car of all is the caboose.

Can you imagine!
Once there were no trains or trucks
or cars or buses.
What was it like then?
People had to walk and carry
what they could.
Some people rode horses.
Horses and oxen pulled wagons.
Farmers needed animals to pull plows.
Horses pulled farm wagons to market.
And there are still some places
in the world where people
travel and work this way.
It's slow and hard.

Cars and buses, trucks and trains,
all have wheels!
Wheels help us move things
that are too heavy or too big to carry.
They help us travel, too.

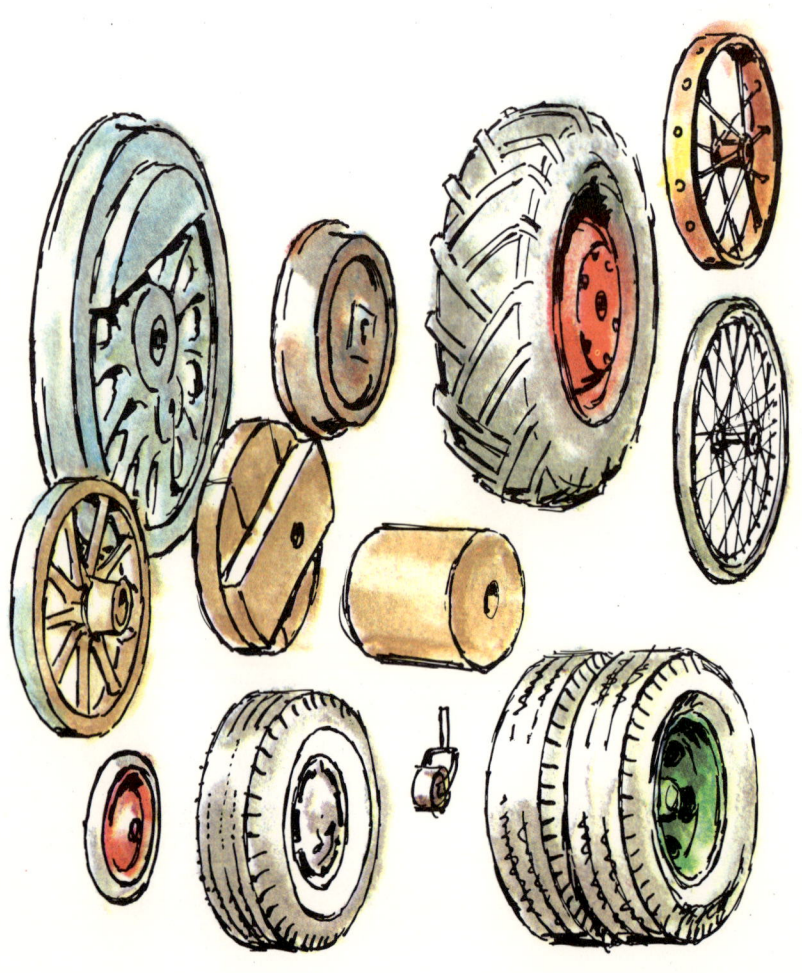

Many toys have wheels—
roller skates, wagons,
toy cars, and doll buggies.
Bicycles and tricycles have wheels, too.
They take you places just for fun.

When we are in a big hurry
we use wings and fly in airplanes.
Planes have wheels to hurry them
into the air.
And these wheels bring the plane
to a safe stop at the end of the trip.

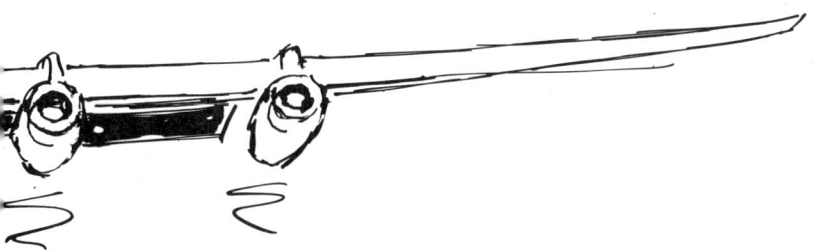

Where do the wheels go when the plane is flying?
They fold up into the plane.

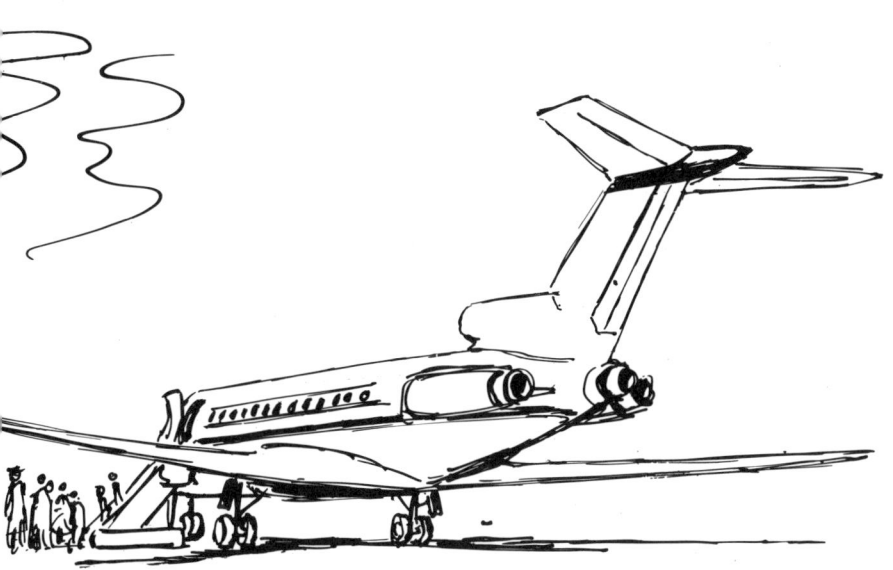

Some big planes carry freight.
These are "flying boxcars."
These planes carry many kinds of freight like food and mail and flowers.

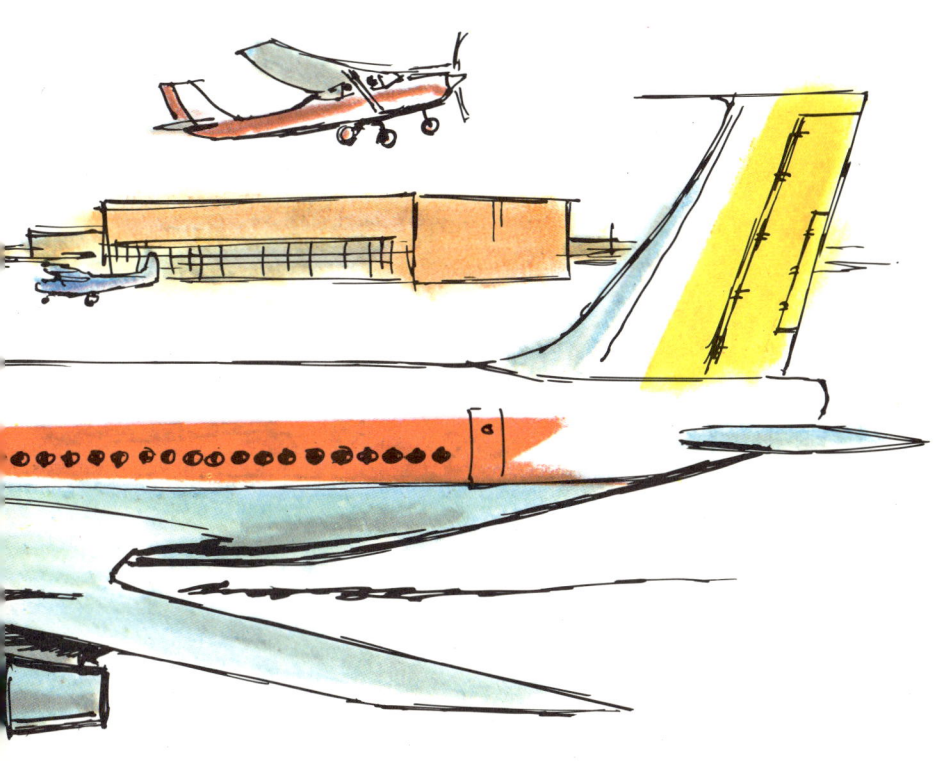

Not all planes are big.
Some families use small planes
just as they do their cars.
Some businessmen fly their own planes, too.
They drive to the airport,
get into their plane, and away they go!

Policemen use helicopters.
They fly low and watch for cars
going too fast.
A policeman in the helicopter
talks over his radio to policemen
on the ground.
Firemen use helicopters, too.
The fire chief gives orders to his men.

Some people fly in helicopters
from the airport to the city.
A helicopter can land in a small space.
It can even land on a roof
or an empty lot.

Wings and wheels!
Where will they take you?
They take Mike and Mary to school
and to play.
They take people to work, to shop,
and to visit.
Safe and fast!
They'll take you there
and home again.